Owlkids Books Inc.
10 Lower Spadina Avenue, Suite 400, Toronto, Ontario M5V 2Z2
www.owlkids.com

Published in France under the title *Raconte-moi les formes, les chiffres, les couleurs* © 2011
Éditions Escabelle, 11 rue Danielle Casanova, 92 500 Rueil Malmaison

Distributed in Canada by University of Toronto Press
5201 Dufferin Street, Toronto, Ontario M3H 5T8

Distributed in the United States by Publishers Group West
1700 Fourth Street, Berkeley, California 94710

Library and Archives Canada Cataloguing in Publication

Gravier-Badreddine, Delphine
    Tell me about colors, shapes, and opposites / written by Delphine
Badreddine ; illustrated by Aurélie Guillerey.

Translation of: Raconte-moi les formes, les chiffres, les couleurs--
ISBN 978-1-926973-54-8

    1. Vocabulary--Juvenile literature. 2. Word recognition--Juvenile
literature. I. Guillerey, Aurélie II. Title.

PE1449.G73 2012   j428.1   C2011-907759-0

Library of Congress Control Number: 2011943506

Translator: Lesley Zimic

We acknowledge the financial support of the Canada Council for the Arts, the Ontario Arts Council, the
Government of Canada through the Canada Book Fund (CBF) and the Government of Ontario through
the Ontario Media Development Corporation's Book Initiative for our publishing activities.

Manufactured by Toppan Leefung Packaging & Printing (Dongguan) Co., Ltd.
Manufactured in Dongguan, China, in June 2012
Job #117094-1

A   B   C   D   E   F

Publisher of Chirp, chickaDEE and OWL
www.owlkids.com

Tell Me About Colors, Shapes, and Opposites

Delphine
Badreddine

Aurélie
Guillerey

What's Inside?

Where are you hiding?

What are you doing?

What colors do you see?

What shapes do you see?

Will you come to our party?

When are you going?

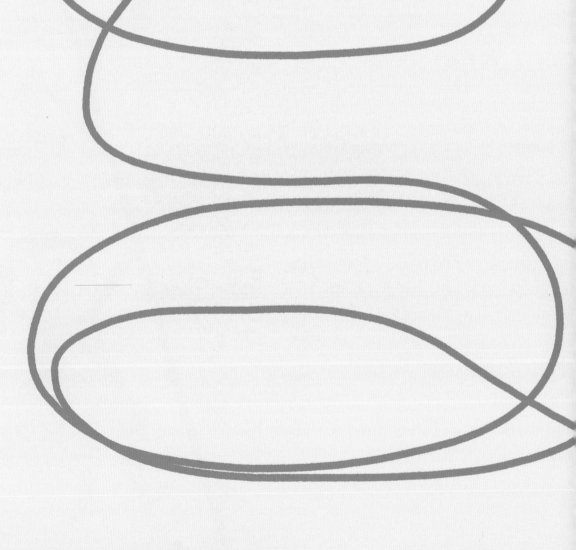

Above

Below

On the top

On the bottom

Just beside

On the left

In the middle

On the right

Inside

Outside

Behind

In front

What are you doing?

Small   Medium

Big

Re

Thin

Short

Thick

Long

Twisted

Leaning

Straight

What colors do you see?

Black

Gray

White

Green

Dark brown

Light brown

Dark green

Light green

Blue

Pink

Purple

What shapes do you see?

Checks

Loops

Dots

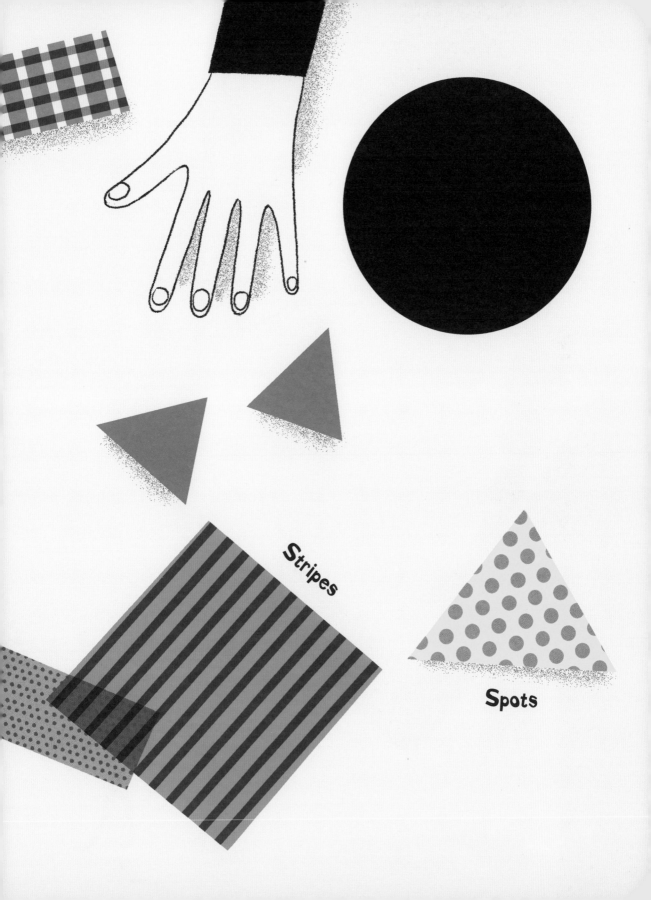

Stripes

Spots

Will you come to our party?

Alone

Together

In a line

Two by two

The whole thing

A piece

A section

A slice

Many

Still a few

None at all

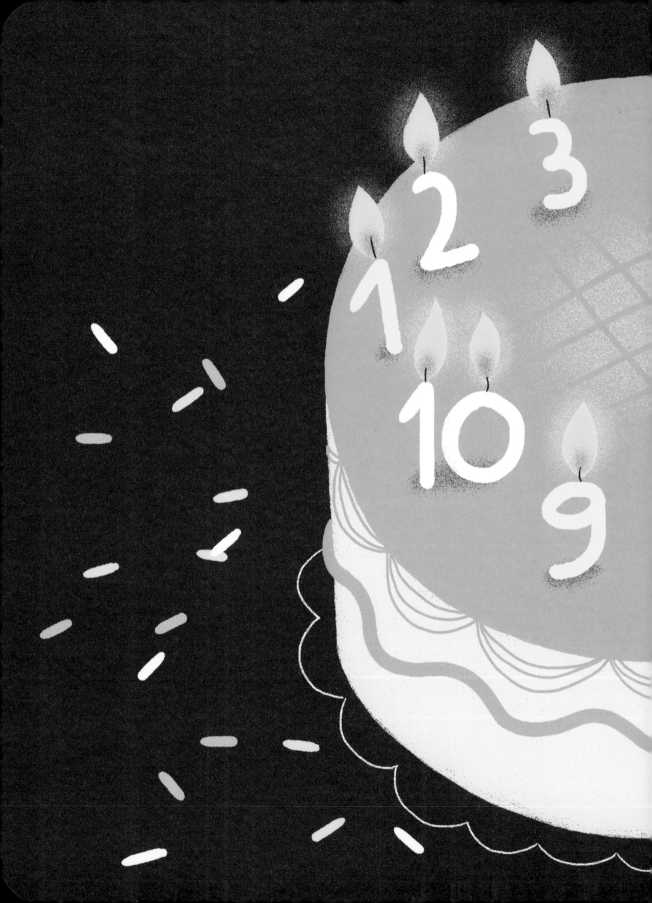

When are you going?

Morning

Evening

Before

During

After